BASKETBALL

by Will Graves

Early Encyclopedias

An Imprint of Abdo Reference
abdobooks.com

abdobooks.com

Published by Abdo Reference, a division of ABDO, PO Box 398166, Minneapolis, Minnesota 55439. Copyright © 2024 by Abdo Consulting Group, Inc. International copyrights reserved in all countries. No part of this book may be reproduced in any form without written permission from the publisher. Early Encyclopedias™ is a trademark and logo of Abdo Reference.

052023
092023

Editor: Charlie Beattie
Series Designers: Candice Keimig, Joshua Olson

Library of Congress Control Number: 2022949123

Publisher's Cataloging-in-Publication Data

Names: Graves, Will, author.
Title: Basketball / by Will Graves
Description: Minneapolis, Minnesota: Abdo Reference, 2024 | Series: Early sports encyclopedias | Includes online resources and index.
Identifiers: ISBN 9781098291266 (lib. bdg.) | ISBN 9781098277444 (ebook)
Subjects: LCSH: Basketball--Juvenile literature. | Basketballers--Juvenile literature. | Team sports--Juvenile literature. | Sports--History--Juvenile literature. | Encyclopedias and dictionaries--Juvenile literature.
Classification: DDC 796.03--dc23

CONTENTS

Introduction 4
    The Game 6
    Skills 20
    Positions 28
    History 42
    The Sport Today 58
    Top NBA Teams 72
    Top WNBA Teams 82
    Top Men's College Teams 88
    Top Women's College Teams 94
    Icons 98

Glossary 126
To Learn More 127
Index 127
Photo Credits 128

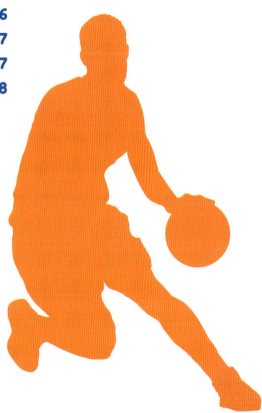

INTRODUCTION

In 1891, students at a Massachusetts school needed a game to play in the winter. So physical education teacher Dr. James Naismith created one. He called his new sport "basket ball." His original game had 13 rules. Players shot the ball into a peach basket.

Dr. James Naismith holds up an early basketball and peach basket hoop.

Superstars like Elena Delle Donne, *right*, have helped make basketball one of the world's most popular games.

Since then, the name has changed to "basketball." The peach basket has changed. It is now a wire rim with a fabric net. The game has also become one of the most popular sports in the world. In 2020, more than 450 million people played basketball.

THE GAME

Two teams line up before the start of a game.

How It Works

Basketball is played on a rectangular court. It has a hoop at each end. Each game has two teams of up to five players. The goal of each team is to get the ball through the opponent's hoop as many times as it can.

Basketball is a fast-moving sport. The team that has the ball is on offense. The team without the ball is on defense. Every player plays both. Because of this, basketball players are excellent athletes.

> **Jumping Center**
>
> A basketball game begins with an opening tip-off. One player from each team stands at center court. An official throws the ball into the air. Two players jump and try to knock it to a teammate.

Teams are awarded two points for most made baskets. Shots taken behind the three-point line are worth three. Free throws are worth one point. The team with the most points at the end of a game wins.

A player dribbles against a defender.

THE GAME

The Court

A full-size basketball court is 94 feet (29 m) from end to end. It is 50 feet (15 m) wide. On each side is a small out-of-bounds area. The court is divided in half by the half-court line. Each half looks the same. The painted area, or "lane," stretches from under the basket to the free-throw line.

Each half also has one or more three-point lines painted. The three-point line sits at different distances depending on the age of the players. Youth and high school players shoot from a line that is 19 feet, 9 inches (6 m) away from the basket. College and Women's National Basketball Association (WNBA) players use a line that is 22 feet, 1.75 inches (6.8 m). National Basketball Association (NBA) players shoot three-pointers from 23 feet, 9 inches (7.2 m) away.

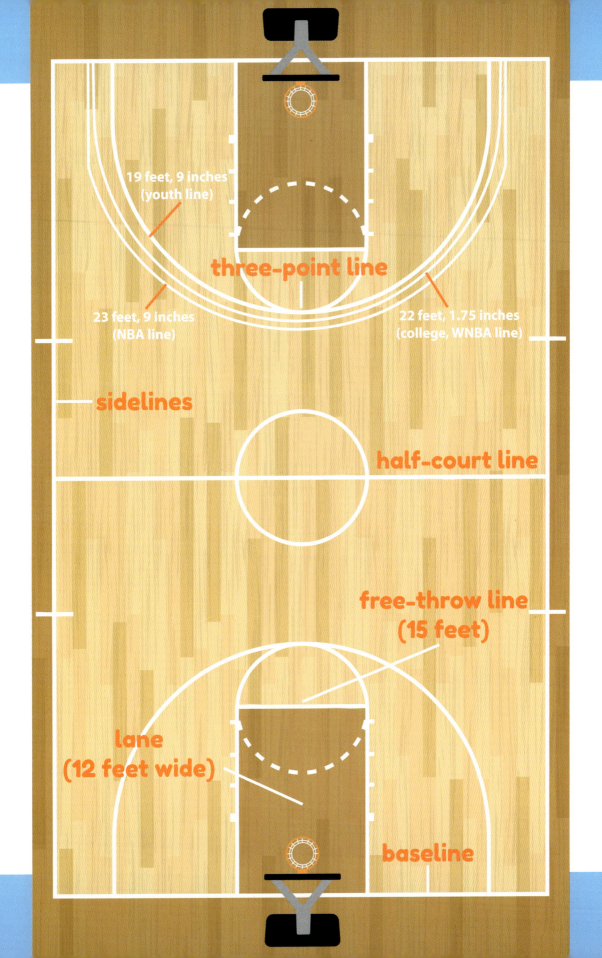

THE GAME

The Ball

Basketballs can be made of different types of materials. The type of ball players use depends on where the game is being played. Most indoor games are played with a leather basketball. They are softer than other types of basketballs. That makes them easier to grip. Rubber basketballs are better for playing games outside. They are

Most indoor basketballs are dark orange or light brown.

a little bit tougher. Rubber balls don't get worn down by playing on hard surfaces like cement.

Balls also come in different sizes. Younger players and most women's players use a ball that is 28.5 inches (72.4 cm) around. Players ages 13 and up use a bigger ball that measures 29.5 inches (74.9 cm) around.

Using a smaller ball helps young players master controlling it while they are still growing.

THE GAME

Uniforms

In a basketball game, the players run a lot. Their uniforms are designed to make it easy for them to move. The uniforms are made of light fabrics. That helps players stay cool while they play.

Basketball jerseys are lightweight and allow players to move quickly.

Some players wear extra gear such as knee sleeves to help protect their bodies.

Uniforms are made up of a jersey and shorts. Most jerseys do not have sleeves. Players must tuck their jerseys into their shorts during official games.

The length of the shorts has changed over time. At some points, players have worn them very short. At other times, they have draped just below players' knees. Most players wear them somewhere in between.

Players also wear socks and specially designed shoes for games. Players can also wear goggles, headbands, wristbands, knee sleeves, full-sleeve undershirts, and tights over their legs.

THE GAME

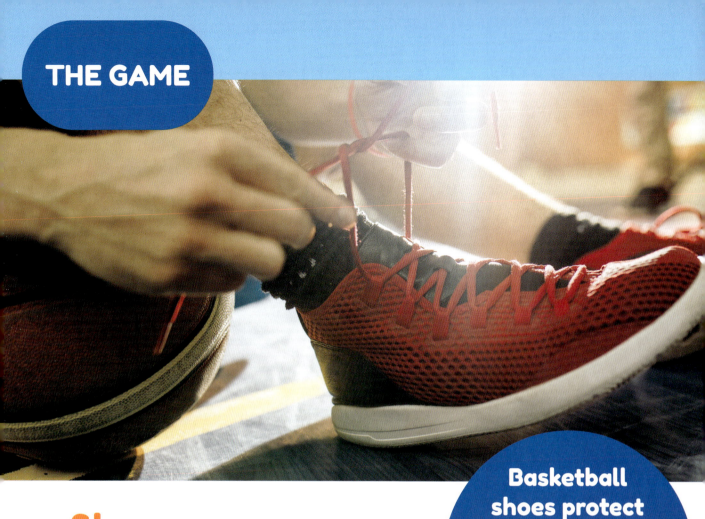

Shoes

Basketball shoes are designed to support players' feet while they run, cut, and jump. The shoes have soft material inside. Sticky soles help players stop on the court. Basketball shoes come in high-top and low-top styles. High-top shoes go above a player's ankle. Each player chooses which type

> Basketball shoes protect players' feet and help with both jumping and stopping on the court.

of shoes they like to wear. The first popular basketball shoes were called All-Stars. They were made by the Converse shoe company starting in the 1910s. Later they were renamed Chuck Taylor All-Stars. By the 1970s and 1980s, other companies like Nike, Reebok, and Adidas started making their own shoes.

Today many professional players work with these companies to design their own lines of shoes. Many people wear basketball shoes every day, not only when playing.

FUN FACT!

Michael Jordan was one of the first basketball players to design his own shoe. The first Air Jordans were worn in 1984.

The Chuck Taylor was the most popular basketball shoe for decades.

THE GAME

Team Makeup

Basketball teams are made up of anywhere from five to 15 players. Five players are on the court at a time. Other players wait on the bench until a coach sends them into the game. Teams can make substitutions to keep their players fresh. Coaches also substitute certain players for different situations.

A team's starting five huddles together before taking the court.

The Swedish men's national basketball team poses for a team photo.

Most teams have two guards, two forwards, and one center on the court. Guards usually play farther from the basket. They also handle the ball more. Forwards and centers usually play closer to the hoop. Their height is a bigger advantage there.

Teams don't need to use two guards, two forwards, and a center. For example, some teams play with an extra guard and no center.

THE GAME

Coaches often use time-outs to talk strategy or motivate their players.

Coaching and Plays

Offenses often use set plays. Coaches try to get certain players open for certain shots. Most plays will have more than one choice. That way the ball can go to whoever is open.

There are two main half-court defensive strategies. The first is man-to-man defense.

University of Connecticut women's coach Geno Auriemma, *right*, shouts instructions during a game.

In man-to-man, each defender guards one opponent. Players will usually guard a player who is the same height and size as them.

The other option is zone defense. In zone, players guard an area of the court. Anytime the ball enters that area, the defender needs to be active.

Coaches can also set up defenses that cover the whole court. These are called full-court presses. They are used to put pressure on the other team and hopefully get the ball. Full-court defenses are usually used when a team is losing and wants to catch up.

SKILLS

Shooting

Jump shots, layups, and dunks are the three main types of shots. Jump shots are taken farther from the basket. A player leaps off the ground. At the same time, he pushes the ball toward the basket with his arms and wrists. The player uses his "shooting hand" to push the ball. He holds his other hand steady to guide the shot.

It's best for a player to release his jump shot near the top of his jump.

Layups are shots taken near the basket. A player softly rolls the ball underhand either off the backboard or straight into the hoop.

Georgeann Wells was the first woman to dunk in a game. She did so while playing for West Virginia University in 1984.

Many fans think the dunk is the most exciting shot in basketball. A dunk is like a layup. But a player uses one or two hands to force the ball through the hoop. Players have to be able to get their hands above the rim and grab it. This usually means jumping high into the air. Not all players can dunk.

No Dunks Allowed

The slam dunk used to be against the rules in college basketball. The shot was illegal for nine years in the 1960s and 1970s. It was thought to be too easy for taller players.

SKILLS

Passing

Passing is the fastest way for teams to move the ball. The chest pass is the most common pass in basketball. To make a chest pass, a player holds the ball at her chest with two hands. She then steps toward her target and pushes the ball where she wants it to go.

A bounce pass is used when defenders are blocking the passing lanes. The passer aims at a spot on the floor near her teammate. The goal is to have the ball bounce off the floor so her teammate can grab it at her waist.

Other types of passes include the overhead pass and the baseball pass. Overhead passes are thrown with two hands. They are usually done to get the ball over a defender. Baseball passes are one-armed throws. They are used to toss the ball long distances down the floor.

University of Iowa point guard Caitlin Clark executes a chest pass during the 2023 NCAA tournament.

SKILLS

Dribbling and Ballhandling

A player cannot run with the ball for more than two steps in basketball. If they want to go any farther, they must dribble.

Louisiana State University forward Angel Reese dribbles the ball during the 2023 NCAA tournament.

Players dribble by bouncing the ball off the floor as they move. Players can dribble the ball with only one hand at a time. They are allowed to switch hands, but the ball has to bounce in between each hand touching it. If a player stops dribbling, they cannot start again.

If a player takes three steps or more without dribbling, that is called "traveling." If a player travels, the ball is awarded to the other team. Players must also keep the hand they are dribbling with above the ball. If they do not, it is a "palming" violation.

FUN FACT!

James Naismith's original basketball rules said that players could only move the ball by passing it. In 1901, the rules were changed. Players were now allowed to dribble once. Unlimited dribbling was not allowed until 1909.

SKILLS

Staying in a low defensive stance helps a player move and stay in front of his opponent.

Defense

Defense starts with a good stance. A player must bend his legs, extend his arms, and crouch down just a little. Players who play good defense make sure they move when their opponents move. They do this by quickly shuffling their feet in the same direction their opponent is going. The key to being a good defender is playing with great effort and control.

A defender's main job is to stop an opponent from scoring. But defenders can also try to make steals or block shots. They must do both without touching the offensive player. If a defender does so, he can be called for a foul.

An Ohio State player blocks a shot during a game against Penn State.

POSITIONS

Point Guard

The point guard is a team's main ballhandler. This player is usually the one who brings the ball up the floor and starts a possession. A coach will usually call a play. But a point guard will pass it on to the rest of the team.

Chicago Sky point guard Courtney Vandersloot, *left*, averaged a career-high ten assists per game in 2020.

At his peak, Russell Westbrook was an excellent passer, scorer, and rebounder.

On offense, a point guard's main job is to break down the defense. They can do this by either passing to teammates or dribbling past defenders. Point guards are often the shortest players on the floor. Many times they are the quickest too.

Some point guards are good scorers. But many focus on passing first. A team's point guard almost always has the most assists.

POSITIONS

Shooting Guard

The other guard on a team is known by many names. Some people call the position the "two guard." Others call it the "off guard." Most people call it the "shooting guard."

The shooting guard is usually a team's best outside shooter. Her job is to get open for shots anywhere she can. The best shooting guards can also drive to the basket and create easy layup or dunk shots. Shooting guards who can do both are very dangerous scorers.

Klay Thompson is one of the best shooting guards in NBA history.

A shooting guard that can hit outside shots can also help teammates score. Defenders will not want to leave a good shooting guard open. That means they can't help guard bigger players inside. This way, the shooting guard opens up space for forwards.

Shooting guard Kelsey Plum averaged 20.2 points per game in 2022 for the WNBA champion Las Vegas Aces.

POSITIONS

Small Forward

Most small forwards can do a little bit of everything. They are usually the shortest of the forwards on the floor. Good small forwards are comfortable playing both close to and away from the basket. Many small forwards are also good ballhandlers.

On defense, small forwards can often guard bigger players. A small forward can use his quickness to bother a center or power forward. He can also use his height to cause problems for smaller guards.

Some coaches call their small forwards "stretch" forwards. That's because coaches ask

The Point Forward

Many small forwards have been good passers and ballhandlers. Players of this size who dribble and pass a lot have been called "point forwards." Players like Larry Bird, Magic Johnson, and LeBron James have played this role.

the small forwards to play far from the basket. That "stretches" the floor to create space for their teammates.

Kevin Durant's height, quickness, and shooting ability make him a great scorer as a small forward.

POSITIONS

Power Forward

Power forwards are some of the tallest and strongest players on the floor. They are usually asked to play near the basket. There they battle with other big and strong players for rebounds.

Power forwards also try to block shots. They help their teammates when a smaller player beats their defender and gets close to the basket. Power forwards slide over and try to stop the offensive player from getting to the basket.

Power forward Breanna Stewart, *left*, has averaged more than 20 points per game and eight rebounds per game in her WNBA career.

Kevin Garnett was one of the first power forwards to play both outside and inside.

On offense, power forwards used to play like centers. They would stay close to the basket and take short shots. Many power forwards now have good outside shooting skills. It is common to see power forwards taking three-point shots today.

POSITIONS

Former NBA center Yao Ming, *left*, stood 7 feet, 6 inches tall.

Center

Centers are almost always the tallest players on the court. They try to use that height on both ends of the floor. Centers almost always play close to the basket. On offense, they can get easy shots or dunks. On defense, they can block shots. Because of their size and strength, good centers can be tough to beat.

Centers need to be good rebounders. On defense, they can grab missed shots and start possessions for their team. On offense, they can keep possessions alive. Grabbing an offensive rebound can lead to a good scoring chance.

Sylvia Fowles, *right*, blocked 721 shots during her 15 years in the WNBA.

POSITIONS

Sixth Man

It takes more than five good players to win a basketball game. For many teams, the first player to come off the bench is very important.

The first substitute is called "the sixth man" or "sixth player." The role rose to fame in the 1940s. A coach named Red Auerbach figured out it would help the team if one of his best players started the game on the bench. Then he could bring him in when the other team's starters were tired.

Tyler Herro of the Miami Heat won the NBA's Sixth Man of the Year Award in 2021–22.

DeWanna Bonner won the WNBA's Sixth Player of the Year Award three times from 2009 to 2011.

Auerbach was right. Soon other teams began using "sixth men." The NBA and WNBA now give out awards to the Sixth Man and Sixth Player of the Year.

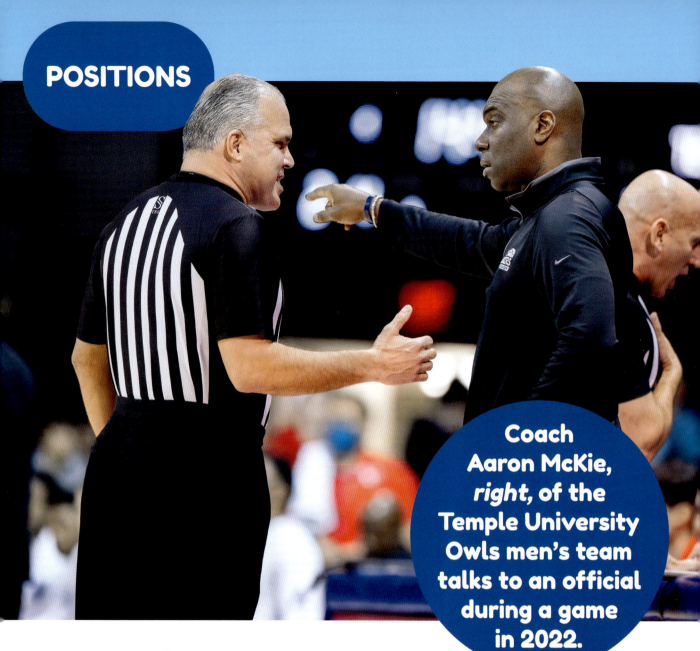

POSITIONS

Coach Aaron McKie, *right*, of the Temple University Owls men's team talks to an official during a game in 2022.

Coach

A coach is the leader of a basketball team. This person is also the team's teacher. The coach creates schedules and runs practices. The coach also leads the team during games.

In practice, a coach teaches players the basic skills of the game. The coach also designs the strategy and game plan for each game.

During games, coaches tell the players which plays to call on offense. They also decide how the team will play defense. If a team is struggling, its coach can call a time-out. During time-outs, a coach might tell the team to try a different strategy.

Every head coach also has several assistants. Some assistants have special jobs. Many of them design a team's offensive or defensive plans.

Many Jobs

Basketball coaches at different levels have many jobs. Youth and high school coaches focus on teaching basic skills. College coaches manage the games. But they also have to convince players to play at their schools. This is called recruiting. Professional coaches mainly handle strategy.

HISTORY

Origins of Basketball

Basketball began in 1891 in Springfield, Massachusetts. Dr. James Naismith was a teacher who needed an indoor game for his students to play in the winter. Men picked up the game quickly. Women began playing the next year.

During World War I (1914–18), soldiers who had been hurt in battle played the game while they got better. The soldiers then took the game back to their home countries when the war was over.

Dr. James Naismith's original 1891 rules for basketball were typed on these two pieces of paper.

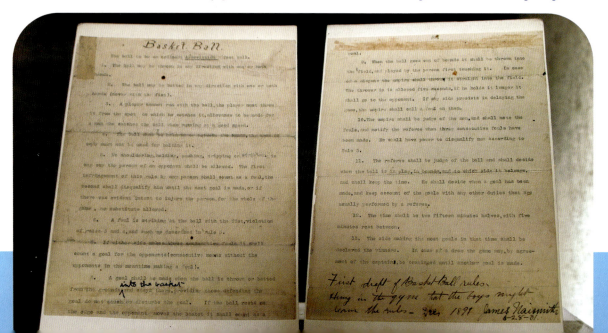

Naismith, *second row, right*, is pictured with his first basketball team.

Basketball made its way to the Olympic Games in 1904. Men's basketball became a permanent part of the Olympics in 1936. Women's basketball joined the Olympics in 1976.

FUN FACT!

Many American soldiers became paralyzed due to injuries they received in World War II (1939–45). They used wheelchairs to move around Many started playing basketball. Wheelchair basketball eventually became a Paralympic sport in 1960.

HISTORY

Early Professional Leagues

Many of the early professional leagues played in the northeastern United States. The first

The Original Celtics were one of many barnstorming professional teams in the early 1900s.

professional league was called the National Basketball League (NBL). The NBL started with six teams in 1898 and lasted five years.

Many other leagues popped up during the first half of the 1900s. The American Basketball League (ABL) was one of the most important early leagues. The ABL ran from 1925 to 1931. It included a New York team called the Original Celtics. They were one of basketball's first great teams. They were so good the ABL forced the team to split up.

The Harlem Globetrotters

One of the most famous basketball teams of all time is a traveling team known as the Harlem Globetrotters. The team started in 1926. Since then it has traveled the world thrilling fans with its entertaining style of play. It combines real basketball with tricks the team's players have mastered.

HISTORY

The University of Oregon beat Ohio State University 46–33 in the 1939 NCAA Championship game.

Men's College Basketball History

The first real game between two colleges was played on February 9, 1895. Minnesota State School of Agriculture beat Hamline University 9–3. Schools from all over the country started to play soon after. Many schools joined conferences.

In 1939, the National Collegiate Athletic Association (NCAA) began holding a year-ending

Dr. James Naismith eventually moved out of Springfield and started the men's basketball program at the University of Kansas.

tournament. Today the NCAA men's tournament is one of the biggest sporting events in the United States. It takes place in March every year. Because of this, it is known as "March Madness" by sports fans.

FUN FACT!

The NCAA men's tournament was not the first major college basketball tournament. The National Invitational Tournament (NIT) began in 1938. The finals were played at Madison Square Garden in New York City. The men's and women's NITs now feature teams that do not make the NCAA tournaments.

HISTORY

Women's College Basketball History

The first women's college game took place in 1896. Stanford University played the University of California. Many schools created teams, but the sport was not as organized as the men's game. Women often played by different rules. Dribbling was even outlawed for women for a short time in the 1910s.

Women play basketball at New York University in the 1930s.

After years of growth, the Women's Final Four is now a huge event held at modern stadiums like Amalie Arena in Tampa, Florida.

It wasn't until the 1970s that women's college basketball started to grow. It took off in the 1980s when the NCAA began hosting a women's tournament. Today the game is very popular. Nearly 6 million fans watched the 2022 NCAA women's tournament championship game.

HISTORY

Before moving to Los Angeles, the Minneapolis Lakers were one of the first great NBA teams in the early 1950s.

NBA History

The NBA was officially born in 1946. The league started with 11 teams. It slowly grew over time. Stars like center George Mikan and point guard Bob Cousy helped the league gain fans in the 1950s. By the 1960s, the NBA had teams all over the country.

In the 1980s, the NBA boomed. Superstars like Magic Johnson and Larry Bird drew in fans.

Rival League

The American Basketball Association (ABA) tried to challenge the NBA in the 1960s and 1970s. The ABA allowed the three-point shot and created the Slam Dunk Contest. The ABA did not last. But four of its teams survived to join the NBA in 1976. They were the Denver Nuggets, Indiana Pacers, New York Nets, and San Antonio Spurs.

So did Michael Jordan. Today the NBA is one of the most popular sports leagues in the world. Its stars come from all over the globe.

Barclays Center in Brooklyn, which opened in 2012, is one of the NBA's newest arenas.

HISTORY

WNBA History

The WNBA was founded in 1996. The league began playing in eight cities in the summer of 1997. The first WNBA teams all played in cities where the NBA already had a team.

The WNBA has now expanded to places like Las Vegas, Nevada, and Hartford, Connecticut.

The early days of the WNBA were dominated by the Houston Comets. The Comets won each of the first four WNBA titles.

Many teams struggled for money in the early years. Some stopped playing completely. But the league survived. The WNBA grew into the most well-known professional women's basketball league in the world.

The Los Angeles Sparks and New York Liberty played the first WNBA game on June 21, 1997. New York won 67–57.

HISTORY

The 1936 United States men's Olympic basketball team beat Canada 19–8 in the gold medal game.

Men's International Basketball History

Basketball spread all over the world soon after it was invented. In the 1930s, the International Basketball Federation (FIBA) was founded. The first countries to join FIBA included Greece and Italy. Men's basketball became an Olympic sport in 1936. The United States won every gold medal in Olympic play until 1972.

In 1992, many of the NBA's best stars competed for Team USA in Barcelona, Spain. The "Dream Team" dominated. Fans around the world were drawn to the star-studded team. That helped basketball grow in many countries. Today, some of the best male players were born outside the United States.

FUN FACT!

Men's basketball has also played a World Cup since 1950. The United States won its fifth gold medal at the tournament in 2014.

The "Dream Team" collects its medals at the 1992 Olympics.

HISTORY

Women's International Basketball History

Women have played basketball nearly as long as men. But they haven't had the same opportunities. Some of the men who organized sports believed they were not proper for women. That slowly began to change. A world championship tournament for women was first played in 1953. Today, it is called the FIBA Women's World Cup.

United States guard Kim Mulkey, *left*, drives for a layup against Canada at the 1984 Olympics in Los Angeles.

Women's basketball joined the Summer Olympics in 1976. The first tournament was won by the Soviet Union. Team USA won its record seventh Olympic gold medal in a row in 2021.

Americans Skylar Diggins-Smith, *left*, Diana Taurasi, *center*, and Brittney Griner pose with their medals after winning the Olympic tournament in Tokyo, Japan, in 2021.

THE SPORT TODAY

NBA Season

The NBA plays an 82-game regular season. The season starts in October and runs through mid-April. Each of the NBA's 30 teams plays 41 games at home. Each one also plays 41 games on the road. Every team plays all of the others at least twice during the season.

The NBA is divided up into six divisions and two conferences. They are based on geography. The Atlantic, Southeast, and Central divisions are in the Eastern Conference. The Northwest, Southwest, and Pacific Divisions are in the Western Conference.

One of the highlights of the NBA season is All-Star Weekend. It includes a 3-point contest and a Slam Dunk Contest. The next night, the league's best players play each other.

Map of NBA Teams

THE SPORT TODAY

The Toronto Raptors celebrate their victory over the Golden State Warriors in the 2019 NBA Finals.

NBA Playoffs and Finals

The NBA playoffs start in mid-April. They end in June. The eight best teams in each conference make the playoffs.

There are four rounds to the NBA playoffs. Every round is played in a best-of-seven series. The first team to win four games moves on.

The winners of the Eastern Conference and Western Conference meet in the NBA Finals. The winner of the finals is crowned NBA champion for that season.

FUN FACT!

The NBA champion wins the Larry O'Brien Trophy. O'Brien was the league's commissioner from 1975 to 1984.

The Larry O'Brien Trophy is made of more than 15 pounds (7 kg) of sterling silver and gold.

THE SPORT TODAY

WNBA Season

The WNBA season is played during the summer. The regular season begins in May. It ends in September. The playoffs come after the regular season.

The length of the WNBA season has grown many times. The first season was 28 games. In 2023, the WNBA expanded the schedule to 40 games per team.

The WNBA hosts an All-Star Game in the middle of each season. The All-Star Game is played in a different WNBA city each year. Like the NBA, the weekend has a three-point contest. It also has a Skills Challenge.

Year-Round Players

WNBA players play a much shorter season than NBA players. They also don't make as much money. Because of this, many WNBA players go to other countries during the winter. They play a second season for another team.

Map of WNBA Teams

THE SPORT TODAY

WNBA Playoffs

The WNBA playoffs are held at the end of each regular season. The eight teams with the best records during the season qualify for the playoffs.

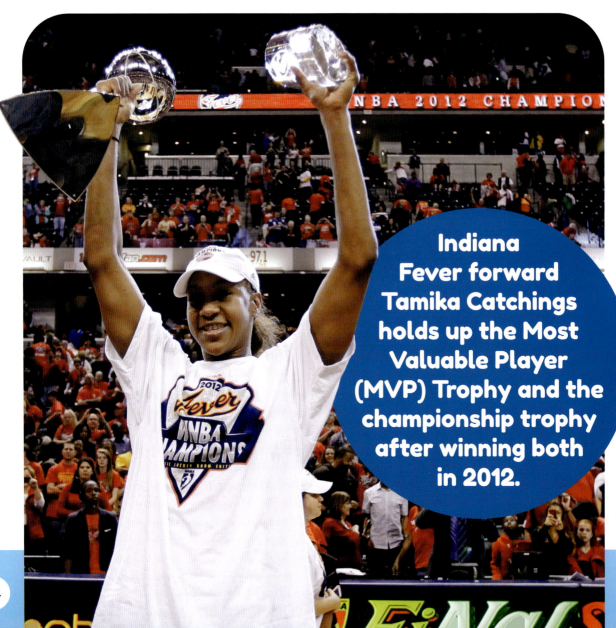

Indiana Fever forward Tamika Catchings holds up the Most Valuable Player (MVP) Trophy and the championship trophy after winning both in 2012.

The Las Vegas Aces pose with the championship trophy after winning the 2022 WNBA Finals.

The playoffs are divided into three rounds. The first round is a best-of-three series. The semifinals and finals are best-of-five series. The winner of the finals is named WNBA champions for that season.

FUN FACT!

The WNBA playoffs have changed many times. From 2016 to 2021, the playoffs lasted four rounds. The teams with the two best records in the league didn't have to play in either of the first two rounds. Those rounds were single games to knock out the other teams.

THE SPORT TODAY

Duke University, *left*, and the University of Virginia tip off in a 2012 men's game.

College Basketball Season

College basketball's season starts in November. It runs through early March. Teams are divided into conferences. Most conferences are based on schools that are close to each other.

There are more than 350 Division I men's teams. That is the top level of college basketball. There are also roughly 350 women's teams. They are spread out over 32 conferences. Most teams play about 30 games during the regular season.

Most conferences have a tournament at the end of the regular season. The winner gets a place in the NCAA tournament.

University of South Carolina forward Aliyah Boston dribbles during a women's game in December 2022.

THE SPORT TODAY

NCAA Tournament

The NCAA tournaments start in March. They are played over three weekends. They usually end in early April. Both the men's and women's tournaments have 68 teams. They include 32 conference champions and 36 "at-large" teams. Those are chosen based on how well they played during the season.

After the first round, the teams are put into four 16-team regions. The winners of the four regions reach the semifinals. This is known as

Louisiana State University celebrates after winning the 2023 NCAA women's championship.

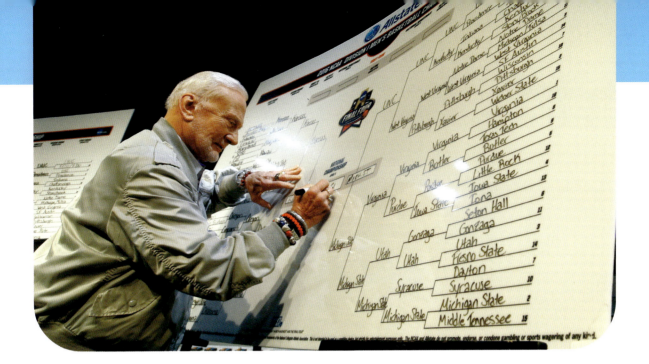

Former astronaut Buzz Aldrin fills out a bracket before the 2015 men's NCAA tournament.

the "Final Four." The winner of the tournament is the national champion.

The tournaments have become famous for their upsets. Fans all over the world try to pick who will win each game. Filling out an NCAA tournament bracket is a favorite tradition.

Cutting the Nets

At the end of every national championship game, the winning team cuts down the net with a pair of scissors. That began in 1947 when the men's coach at North Carolina State University cut down the nets after his team won a big tournament.

THE SPORT TODAY

The Olympics

Every four years, teams from different countries play each other at the Olympics. The Olympic men's and women's basketball tournaments each include 12 teams.

The Olympic tournaments start with a group stage. Each country plays three other countries in that round. The eight teams with the best records advance to the knockout stage. That

US men's guard Kobe Bryant goes up for a dunk during the 2008 Olympics in Beijing, China.

70

Candace Parker, *left*, of the United States tries to block a shot against Croatia at the 2012 Olympics in London, England.

is a single elimination round. The team that wins four games in this round wins the gold medal. The team that loses the final receives the silver medal. The two teams that lost in the semifinals compete for the bronze medal.

Three-on-Three

The Olympics featured three-on-three basketball for the first time in 2020. It is played with just one hoop. Games are played to 21 points. A shot from inside the three-point line is worth one point. A shot made outside the three-point line is worth two points.

71

TOP NBA TEAMS

Boston Celtics

The Boston Celtics are one of the most successful teams in the history of men's pro sports. The Celtics won their 17th title in 2008. That was an NBA record at the time.

The Boston Celtics were founded in 1946. From 1956 to 1969, they won 11 championships in 13 seasons. At one point, they won eight in

The Boston Celtics reached the NBA Finals for the 22nd time in 2022.

a row. Guard Bob Cousy and center Bill Russell led those teams.

The team won two more titles in the 1970s. Forward John Havlicek and center Dave Cowens were the team's stars. In the 1980s, Larry Bird led Boston to three more championships.

The Celtics played their games at Boston Garden until 1995. The old building was famous for its parquet floor. The floor design remained the same after the team moved to a new arena.

John Havlicek's No. 17 jersey was retired by the Celtics to honor him.

TOP NBA TEAMS

Los Angeles Lakers

The Lakers began in Minneapolis in 1947. The team won five NBA titles there. They moved to Los Angeles in 1960. They won again in 1972. That team was led by superstar center Wilt Chamberlain and guard Jerry West.

The Lakers became a powerhouse again in the 1980s. Los Angeles won five titles in the decade. They had superstars Earvin "Magic" Johnson and center Kareem Abdul-Jabbar. They also enjoyed a great rivalry with the

Star guard Jerry West played for the Lakers from 1960 to 1974.

The Lakers and the Celtics have long had one of the NBA's fiercest rivalries.

Boston Celtics. The Lakers of the 1980s were known as "Showtime" for their flashy play.

Los Angeles was great again in the early 2000s. The team won three straight titles with center Shaquille O'Neal and guard Kobe Bryant. The Lakers matched Boston by winning their 17th championship in 2020.

Celebrity Sightings

The Lakers play their games close to Hollywood. Movie stars often attend games. Legendary actor Jack Nicholson is one famous example. He has had courtside seats since the 1970s.

TOP NBA TEAMS

Michael Jordan, *left*, and Phil Jackson helped the Bulls win six championships in eight years during the 1990s.

Chicago Bulls

The Chicago Bulls joined the NBA in 1966. They didn't win much for years. That changed when the team drafted guard Michael Jordan in 1984. By 1991, Chicago was NBA champion. The team dominated the NBA for most of that decade. Jordan became the most famous basketball player in the world.

Led by Jordan and forward Scottie Pippen, Chicago won again in 1992 and 1993. In 1996, the Bulls started another "three-peat." That season, Chicago won a then-record 72 regular-season games. By the end of the 1997–98 season, they had six titles in eight years. After that year, Jordan retired. The Bulls have not won another championship since.

Scottie Pippen dunks in a 1991 game.

TOP NBA TEAMS

San Antonio Spurs

The San Antonio Spurs joined the NBA from the ABA in 1976. For two decades, they didn't win much. In the late 1990s, they became a great team. They also had players from all over the world.

Tim Duncan was born in the US Virgin Islands.

Tim Duncan, *right*, and David Robinson were known as the "twin towers" when they played together for San Antonio.

He combined with fellow big man David Robinson. The pair lead San Antonio to its first title in 1998–99. Soon they were joined by French point guard Tony Parker and Argentine guard Manu Ginobili. Robinson retired in 2003, but the others helped the Spurs win four more titles through 2013–14.

Tony Parker is the Spurs' all-time leader in assists.

TOP NBA TEAMS

Golden State Warriors

The Philadelphia Warriors won what's now known as the first NBA title in 1946–47. They won another in the 1950s. Then they moved across the country to San Francisco. There they changed their name to the Golden State Warriors. They also won another title in 1974–75.

The Warriors dominated the 2010s. They had great three-point shooting from guards Steph

High-scoring guard Rick Barry led the Warriors to the NBA championship in 1975.

The Warriors hold up their trophy after winning the NBA Finals in 2015.

Curry and Klay Thompson. Draymond Green was a great defender under the hoop. Together they won four NBA titles between 2015 and 2022. Superstar Kevin Durant was also on the team for two of those wins, in 2017 and 2018. No team in NBA history has won more than the 73 games the 2015–16 Warriors did.

FUN FACT!

The team was known as the San Francisco Warriors from 1962 to 1971.

TOP WNBA TEAMS

Comets point guard Kim Perrot celebrates Houston's first championship in 1997.

Houston Comets

The Houston Comets were the first great WNBA team. Houston won the league's first four titles from 1997 to 2000. From 1998 to 2000, the Comets won 80 games. They lost only 14.

Houston had three of the league's best players. Guards Cynthia Cooper and Sheryl Swoopes were great scorers. Forward Tina

Thompson added offense and rebounding. But the Comets didn't last. The team ran out of money and had to stop playing after the 2008 season.

The Air Swoopes

Houston Comets star Sheryl Swoopes was the first female player to get her own basketball shoe. Nike released the Air Swoopes in 1996.

Tina Thompson, *left*, Sheryl Swoopes, *center*, and Cynthia Cooper hold up three WNBA championship trophies at the team's 1999 victory parade.

TOP WNBA TEAMS

Minnesota Lynx

The Minnesota Lynx joined the WNBA in 1999. In the team's first 12 seasons, they won only one playoff game. Minnesota improved fast in 2011. The team drafted forward Maya Moore. The Lynx reached the WNBA Finals in six of the next seven years. They won championships in 2011, 2013, 2015, and 2017.

Moore was not the team's only star. Point guard Lindsey Whalen was a college star at

Stars Lindsey Whalen, *left*, and Maya Moore helped the Minnesota Lynx win four WNBA titles.

Seimone Augustus, *left*, was Minnesota's all-time leading scorer when she left the team in 2019.

the University of Minnesota. Whalen came home to join the Lynx in 2010. Minnesota's title teams also featured forwards Seimone Augustus and Rebekkah Brunson and center Sylvia Fowles.

Rebekkah Brunson

Rebekkah Brunson also won a WNBA title in 2005 with the Sacramento Monarchs. She then won four with Minnesota. Brunson was the first WNBA player ever to win five career titles.

TOP WNBA TEAMS

Seattle Storm

In 2002, the WNBA held its first draft lottery. The teams that missed the playoffs had a chance at the top pick. The Seattle Storm won it. They used the pick on University of Connecticut guard Sue Bird.

From that point on, the Storm were a great team. Bird played 19 seasons and led Seattle to four championships. She teamed up with center Lauren Jackson for the first one in 2004. That duo won again in 2010.

After Jackson retired, forward Breanna Stewart

Lauren Jackson won the WNBA MVP Award three times while playing for the Storm.

joined the Storm. The 6-foot-4-inch star helped Seattle win two more titles in 2018 and 2020.

Breanna Stewart, *left*, and Sue Bird hold up the WNBA Championship trophy after Seattle's win in 2020.

TOP MEN'S COLLEGE TEAMS

University of California, Los Angeles (UCLA) Bruins

UCLA was by far the best college basketball team in the late 1960s and early 1970s. The team won nine championships in 11 years from 1965 to 1975. At one point, the Bruins won 88 games in a row. The team was coached by John Wooden. The quiet coach was nicknamed the "Wizard of Westwood" after the area in Los Angeles where the school sits.

UCLA celebrates on the court after winning the 1971 national championship.

Star Anthony Davis helped Kentucky win the national title in 2012 during his only year at the school.

University of Kentucky Wildcats

Kentucky has had several great coaches. Adolph Rupp coached the team from 1930 to 1972. The school's arena is now named after him. He won four national titles. Joe B. Hall, Rick Pitino, Tubby Smith, and John Calipari have also brought titles to the proud fans of Lexington, where the school is located.

TOP MEN'S COLLEGE TEAMS

Legendary North Carolina coach Dean Smith talks to star guard Michael Jordan on the sidelines.

University of North Carolina Tar Heels

North Carolina has many great basketball teams. It also has one of the sport's best rivalries. On one side is the University of North Carolina. The Tar Heels have been to more than 20 Final Fours. They have won six times. Two of those wins came under the legendary Dean Smith. The first of his championships came in 1982. The team won on a late shot by Michael Jordan.

Duke University Blue Devils

Just 10 miles (16 km) away from North Carolina is Duke University. Duke rose to greatness under Mike Krzyzewski in the 1980s. "Coach K" stayed at Duke until 2022. In that time, he won five national championships. Krzyzewski retired as the all-time leader in wins with 1,202. His final game came in the 2022 Final Four. Duke was upset by North Carolina.

FUN FACT!

Duke students often camp out outside Cameron Indoor Stadium the night before games to try to get a seat. The tent city they set up was called "Krzyzewskiville" when Mike Krzyzewski was coaching the team.

Mike Krzyzewski holds up the net after Duke won the 2015 national championship.

TOP MEN'S COLLEGE TEAMS

Kansas's Allen Fieldhouse is one of the most historic basketball arenas in the United States.

Kansas University Jayhawks

Kansas's basketball program was founded by the inventor of the sport. James Naismith moved to Lawrence, Kansas, in 1898. The successful team won its first national title in 1952 under legendary coach Phog Allen. He was a former Jayhawks player under Naismith. Kansas now plays its games in the Allen Fieldhouse.

One of Indiana's many traditions is its red-and-white striped warm-up pants.

Indiana University Hoosiers

Basketball history runs deep in Indiana also. The Hoosiers program started in 1900. Since then, Indiana has made many NCAA tournaments. The 1975–76 Hoosiers team went 32–0 that year under fiery head coach Bobby Knight. They were only the seventh men's team to win an NCAA championship with a perfect record.

Most NCAA Men's Basketball Titles

UCLA — 11	Duke — 5	Kansas — 4
Kentucky — 8	Indiana — 5	Villanova — 3
North Carolina — 6	Connecticut — 5	

TOP WOMEN'S COLLEGE TEAMS

University of Tennessee Lady Volunteers

The University of Tennessee started to win in the 1980s. The Lady Vols won six national titles between 1987 and 1998. The 1997–98 team went a perfect 39–0. It had stars like Chamique Holdsclaw and Tamika Catchings. Coach Pat Summitt led Tennessee for 38 years until she retired in 2012.

Tennessee players carry coach Pat Summitt off the floor after winning the 1991 national championship.

Connecticut celebrates after winning the 2016 national title.

University of Connecticut Huskies

Connecticut won its first championship in 1995. That year, the Huskies beat Tennessee in the final. The Huskies soon took over as college basketball's top team. Under head coach Geno Auriemma, Connecticut won four titles in five years from 2000 to 2004. The Huskies also reached the Final Four every year from 2009 to 2019.

FUN FACT!

Connecticut won a record 111 games in a row at one point. The streak stretched from November 23, 2014, to March 27, 2017. That's a total of 867 days without losing.

TOP WOMEN'S COLLEGE TEAMS

Stanford players celebrate coach Tara VanDerveer's 900th win at the school in January 2019.

Stanford University Cardinal

Stanford University also has a legendary coach. Tara VanDerveer took over before the 1985–86 season. She put in a strong offensive attack. The Cardinal won their first national title in 1989–90. They won again two years later. Stanford finally won again in 2020–21. VanDerveer was still the head coach.

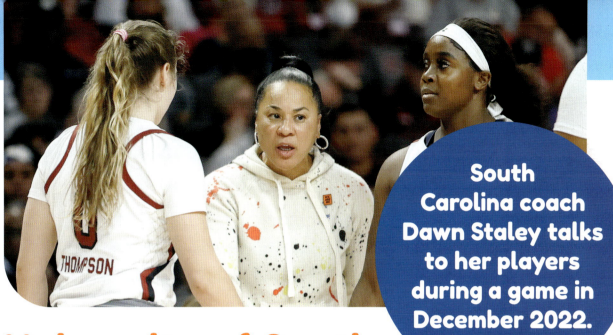

South Carolina coach Dawn Staley talks to her players during a game in December 2022.

University of South Carolina Gamecocks

The University of South Carolina rose to the top of women's basketball using a tough defense. Coach Dawn Staley took over in 2008. She led the Gamecocks to their first title in 2016–17. In 2021–22, they won it again. That year, they held high-powered Connecticut to only 49 points in the championship game.

Most NCAA Women's Basketball Titles

Connecticut – 11	Stanford – 3	Southern California – 2
Tennessee – 8	Louisiana Tech – 2	
Baylor – 3	Notre Dame – 2	South Carolina – 2

ICONS

George Mikan

George Mikan was 6 feet, 10 inches tall. He towered over the rest of the NBA in the 1950s. His dominant play helped the Minneapolis Lakers to five titles in six years. Mikan led the league in scoring three times. He was voted the sport's best player in the first half of the 20th century.

Shot Blocker

George Mikan wasn't just a scorer. In college, he would stand by the rim and swat shots away. The NCAA changed its rules to stop him. The new rule was called goaltending. It still exists today.

George Mikan averaged 23.1 points per game during his seven seasons.

Bob Cousy, *left*, was the NBA MVP in 1956–57.

Bob Cousy

Bob Cousy was one of the best ballhandlers in the early NBA era. The Boston Celtics guard led the league in assists eight times between 1953 and 1960. His fancy dribbling earned him the nickname "Houdini of the Hardwood." He also helped lead the Celtics to win six championships.

ICONS

Bill Russell

Bill Russell was one of the best defensive players in NBA history. He was also a winner. Russell won 11 championships in 13 seasons with the Boston Celtics. A great leader, he was the team's head coach as well as a player for two of those titles. The NBA Finals

Rivals Bill Russell, *right*, and Wilt Chamberlain, *left*, played against each other 143 times during their NBA careers.

Most Valuable Player (MVP) Award is named after Russell.

Wilt Chamberlain

No player ever dominated on offense like Wilt Chamberlain. The 7-foot-1-inch center put up huge numbers. In 1961–62, he averaged 50.4 points per game. That year, he scored 100 points in one game while playing for the Philadelphia Warriors. Only one other NBA player has ever topped 80 points in a game.

Top Single-Game NBA Scorers

100 POINTS
Wilt Chamberlain
Philadelphia Warriors
March 2, 1962

81 POINTS
Kobe Bryant
Los Angeles Lakers
January 22, 2006

78 POINTS
Wilt Chamberlain
Philadelphia Warriors
December 8, 1961

73 POINTS
David Thompson
Denver Nuggets
April 9, 1978

73 POINTS
Wilt Chamberlain
Philadelphia Warriors
January 13, 1962

73 POINTS
Wilt Chamberlain
San Francisco Warriors
November 16, 1962

72 POINTS
Wilt Chamberlain
San Francisco Warriors
November 3, 1962

71 POINTS
Damian Lillard
Portland Trail Blazers
February 26, 2023

71 POINTS
Donovan Mitchell
Cleveland Cavaliers
January 2, 2023

71 POINTS
David Robinson
San Antonio Spurs
April 24, 1994

71 POINTS
Elgin Baylor
Los Angeles Lakers
November 15, 1960

ICONS

Oscar Robertson

Oscar Robertson could score, pass, and rebound. These skills helped him become the king of the triple-double. In 1962, he became the first player to average a triple-double for an entire NBA season. That year, he put up 30.8 points, 12.5 rebounds, and 11.4 assists per game for the Cincinnati Royals.

Oscar Robertson won his only NBA championship with the Milwaukee Bucks in 1971.

Kareem Abdul-Jabbar

Kareem Abdul-Jabbar had the most famous move in NBA history. The 7-foot-2-inch center would float high hook shots. They were called "sky hooks." He used that shot to score a record 38,387 points in his 20-year career. He also won six titles in the 1970s and 1980s with the Milwaukee Bucks and Los Angeles Lakers.

Kareem Abdul-Jabbar attempts a sky hook while playing for the Los Angeles Lakers.

ICONS

Larry Bird

Larry Bird was one of the most skilled forwards the NBA has ever seen. He was tough, a tricky passer, and a great shooter. Bird led the Boston Celtics to three titles in the 1980s. "Larry Legend" averaged more than 20 points, ten rebounds, and six assists in his 13-year career.

Lakers vs. Celtics

Johnson and Bird faced each other in the NBA Finals three times in the 1980s. The rivalry between the teams helped the league become more popular during that decade.

Magic Johnson

Even though Magic Johnson was 6 feet, 9 inches tall, he played point guard. His silky passing led the "Showtime" Lakers to five championships. Johnson could score too. He averaged more than 20 points per game four times between 1979–80 and 1995–96. The always-smiling Johnson was a fan favorite.

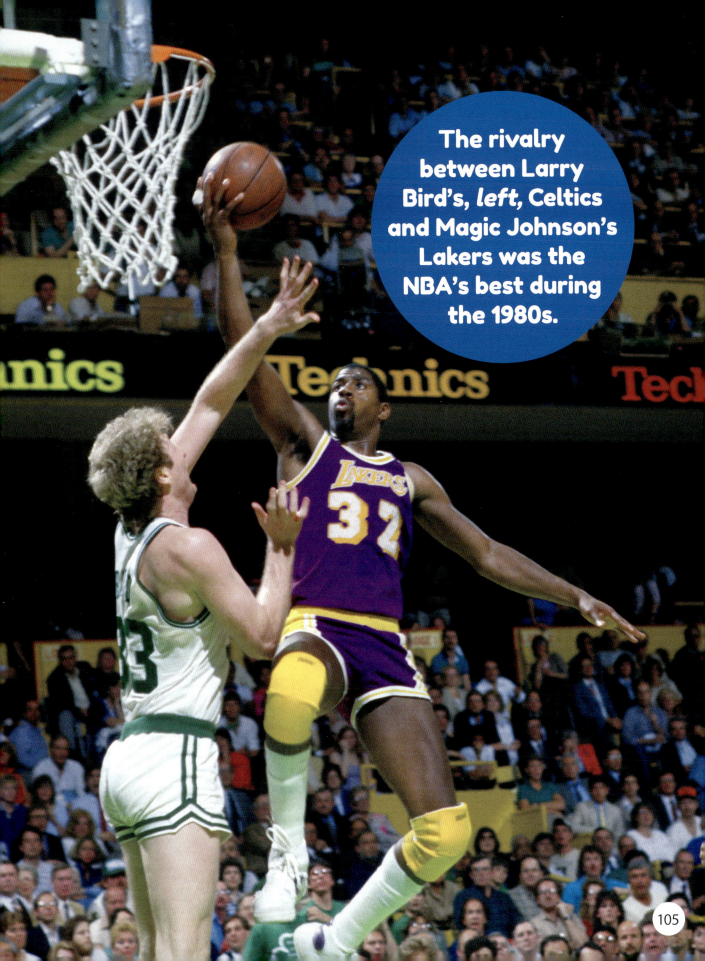

The rivalry between Larry Bird's, *left*, Celtics and Magic Johnson's Lakers was the NBA's best during the 1980s.

ICONS

Michael Jordan

Many fans consider Michael Jordan to be the best player ever. He won six NBA titles in eight years with the Chicago Bulls in the 1990s. Jordan could take over a game with his shooting skill. And his high-flying dunks earned him the nickname "Air Jordan."

Hakeem Olajuwon

Hakeem Olajuwon grew up in Nigeria playing soccer. But when he grew to 7 feet tall, he switched to basketball.

Michael Jordan's series-winning shot in the 1998 NBA Finals is one of the most famous moments in league history.

"The Dream" combined his height and soccer footwork to become a great center. He led the Houston Rockets to championships in 1993–94 and 1994–95.

Hakeem Olajuwon, *center*, led the Rockets to a seven-game NBA Finals win over the New York Knicks in 1994.

ICONS

Shaquille O'Neal

Shaquille O'Neal was so powerful that his dunks sometimes broke backboards. He could also run the floor like a smaller player. That size and speed made him nearly impossible to stop in his 19-year career. O'Neal's best years came with the Lakers. He helped Los Angeles win three straight titles from 1999–2000 to 2001–02.

Los Angeles Lakers center Shaquille O'Neal dunks over a defender during a game in 1998.

Kobe Bryant waves to the crowd after scoring 60 points in his final NBA game in 2016.

Kobe Bryant

One of O'Neal's teammates on those Lakers squads was guard Kobe Bryant. The 6-foot-6-inch Bryant was a terrific scorer. After O'Neal left the Lakers in 2004, Bryant led Los Angeles to two more titles. He retired in 2016 with more than 33,000 NBA points.

ICONS

LeBron James

LeBron James was called the "Chosen One" when he entered the league in 2003. The superstar small forward lived up to the hype. In his first 18 seasons, he led three different teams to NBA championships. That included his hometown Cleveland Cavaliers. James led Cleveland to its first title in 2015–16.

LeBron James became the NBA's all-time leading scorer in 2023.

Steph Curry set an NBA record by hitting 402 three-pointers during the 2015–16 season.

Steph Curry

Steph Curry's record-setting three-point shooting began wowing NBA fans in 2009. In December 2021, Curry became the league's all-time leading three-point shooter. The following spring, he won his fourth NBA championship with the Golden State Warriors.

FUN FACT!

LeBron James and Steph Curry faced each other in four straight NBA Finals from 2015 to 2018. Curry's Warriors won three of the four.

ICONS

Giannis Antetokounmpo

Not many people knew about Giannis Antetokounmpo when the Milwaukee Bucks drafted him in out of Greece in 2013. Six years later, he was the league MVP. The 7-foot forward has the quickness of a guard. In 2020–21, he led the Bucks to their first championship in 50 years.

Giannis Antetokounmpo is known as the "Greek Freak" for his amazing athleticism.

Luka Dončić had 55 triple-doubles in his first 300 NBA games.

Luka Dončić

Luka Dončić has put up amazing statistics during his early NBA career. The Slovenian was the second player born in Europe ever to win NBA Rookie of the Year. In 2019–20, he led the league with 17 triple-doubles. At 21 years old, the guard was the youngest player ever to do that.

ICONS

Red Auerbach was a part of 16 championships with the Boston Celtics as coach, general manager, and team president.

Red Auerbach

Arnold "Red" Auerbach won 938 games coaching the Boston Celtics in the 1950s and 1960s. He used a fast-paced offense to win nine NBA championships. Today the NBA's

Auerbach's Legacy

Black players were discriminated against in the early NBA years. Red Auerbach was the first coach to draft a Black player. He also was the first coach to field an all-Black starting lineup. When he left coaching, Auerbach hired Bill Russell to take his place. Russell was the league's first Black coach.

Coach of the Year Award is called the Red Auerbach Trophy.

Phil Jackson

Phil Jackson led the Chicago Bulls to six championships in the 1990s. The "Zen Master" then moved to Los Angeles and led the Lakers to five more. Along the way, he coached legends like Michael Jordan, Scottie Pippen, Shaquille O'Neal, and Kobe Bryant. Jackson's 11 NBA championships broke Auerbach's record for head coaches.

Phil Jackson talks to Michael Jordan during a game in the 1990s.

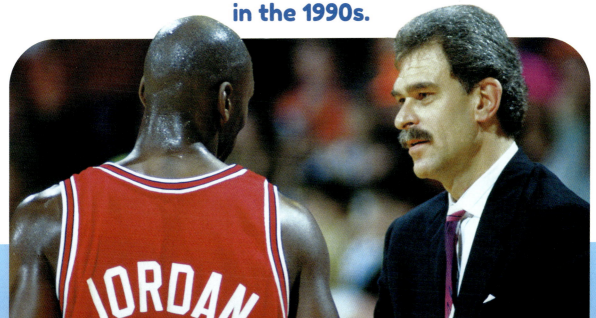

ICONS

Gregg Popovich

Gregg Popovich took over the San Antonio Spurs in 1996. In 2022, he started his 27th season there. Along the way, he set a record for the most wins of all NBA head coaches. Popovich picked up his 1,336th win in March 2022. "Pop" also led the Spurs to five championships.

Gregg Popovich had a winning record in his first 22 full seasons as San Antonio's head coach.

Steve Kerr's positive coaching style has helped the Warriors become an NBA powerhouse.

Steve Kerr

Steve Kerr won championships as a player for both Phil Jackson and Gregg Popovich. He joined them as a great coach when he took over the Golden State Warriors in 2014. Kerr won titles in three of his first four seasons. He also led the 2015–16 Warriors to a record 73 wins.

FUN FACT!

Steve Kerr was a member of the 1995–96 Chicago Bulls when they won an NBA-record 72 games. In 2015–16, he coached the Golden State Warriors team that broke that record.

ICONS

Sheryl Swoopes

Sheryl Swoopes was one of the WNBA's first offensive stars. The Houston Comets guard piled up points with her strong shooting and hard drives to the basket. That style won her three MVP Awards and four WNBA titles.

Sheryl Swoopes, *right*, won the WNBA Defender of the Year Award three times and the league scoring title twice.

Lisa Leslie

The 6-foot-5-inch Lisa Leslie was more than just a great center. Her athleticism made her tough to guard. Leslie played 12 years with the Los Angeles Sparks. She was a great scorer and rebounder. She also made history in 2002. That year she became the first WNBA player to dunk in a game.

Lisa Leslie won the WNBA MVP Award in 2001, 2004, and 2006.

ICONS

Sue Bird

Sue Bird retired in 2022 as the WNBA's all-time leader with 3,234 assists. Those passing skills won her four WNBA titles with the Seattle Storm. Bird also won a lot of international tournaments. She retired as a five-time Olympic gold medalist.

Sue Bird was the first WNBA player to win the league title in three different decades.

Diana Taurasi was named WNBA Finals MVP in 2009 and 2014.

Diana Taurasi

Diana Taurasi and Sue Bird played together at the University of Connecticut. They also teamed up for five Olympic gold medals. Taurasi's shooting made her the WNBA's all-time leading scorer in 2017. She also led the Phoenix Mercury to three championships.

ICONS

Maya Moore played only eight WNBA seasons. Her teams won the league title four times.

Maya Moore

Opposing coaches sometimes called Maya Moore "the Monster." Her clutch shooting scared the teams she played against. That was on display in Game 5 of the 2017 WNBA Finals. Moore's jumper with less than 30 seconds left helped secure the Minnesota Lynx their fourth championship. All of those titles came after Moore joined the team in 2011.

Tamika Catchings

Tamika Catchings was a good offensive player. But she was great on defense. The Indiana Fever forward played 15 years with the team. She won the WNBA's Defensive Player of the Year Award five times. She was also the MVP of the 2012 WNBA Finals when the Fever won their first title.

Tamika Catchings, *right,* makes a steal against Canada during the 2012 Olympics.

ICONS

Breanna Stewart

Breanna Stewart won four NCAA championships in four years at the University of Connecticut. The 6-foot-4-inch Stewart then became a professional star. She won the WNBA MVP Award in 2018. That year, she helped the Seattle Storm win a WNBA title. Stewart helped the Storm win again in 2020.

Breanna Stewart was the MVP of the WNBA Finals in 2018 and 2020 for the Seattle Storm.

A'ja Wilson, *left*, led the Las Vegas Aces to their first WNBA title in 2022.

A'ja Wilson

A'ja Wilson was a star at the University of South Carolina on a championship team in 2017. Like Stewart, the 6-foot-4-inch forward then made a big splash in the WNBA. Wilson was the league's rookie of the year in 2018. She then won two MVP Awards in three years for the Las Vegas Aces.

GLOSSARY

assists
Passes that lead directly to baskets.

clutch
An important or pressure-packed situation.

conference
A group of teams that make up a college league or part of a professional league.

draft
A system that allows teams to acquire new players coming into a league.

foul
Illegal contact with another player during a game.

invent
To create something new.

lane
The area near the basket between the free-throw line and the baseline.

parquet
A wood surface made of patterned square tiles.

rebound
To catch the ball after a shot has been missed.

rookie
A professional athlete in his or her first year of competition.

steal
To take the ball from a player on the other team.

TO LEARN MORE

More Books to Read

Abdo, Kenny. *History of Basketball.* Abdo, 2020.

Abdo, Kenny. *Miracle Moments in Basketball.* Abdo, 2022.

Chandler, Matt. *Basketball Biographies for Kids: The Greatest NBA and WNBA Players from the 1960s to Today.* Rockridge, 2022.

Online Resources

To learn more about basketball, please visit **abdobooklinks.com** or scan this QR code. These links are routinely monitored and updated to provide the most current information available.

INDEX

NBA, 8, 39, 50–52, 55, 58, 60–61, 72, 74, 76, 78, 80–81, 98–104, 106, 109–111, 113–116

NCAA, 46–47, 49, 67–69, 93, 97–98, 124

WNBA, 8, 39, 52, 62, 64–65, 82, 84–86, 118–125

127

PHOTO CREDITS

Cover Photos: Sergey Ryzhov/Shutterstock Images, front (left); Sarah Stier/Getty Images Sport/Getty Images, front (center); Shutterstock Images, front (right, background), back

Interior Photos: Jeff Haynes/AFP/Getty Images, 1, 76, 106; iStockphoto, 3, 14, 20, 61; Historic Collection/Alamy, 4; Keeton Gale/Shutterstock Images, 5, 34; Fabrizio Andrea Bertani/Shutterstock Images, 6, 26; Michele Morrone/Shutterstock Images, 7; Enterline Design/Shutterstock Images, 9; Francesc Juan/Shutterstock Images, 10; Sergey Ryzhov/Shutterstock Images, 11; Bill Kostroun/AP Images, 12; Dmitry Argunov/Shutterstock Images, 13; Shutterstock Images, 15, 49, 51; Dario Zg/Shutterstock Images, 16; Oleksandr Osipov/Shutterstock Images, 17; Matthew Jacques/Shutterstock Images, 18; Debby Wong/Shutterstock Images, 19; Steph Chambers/Getty Images Sport/Getty Images, 23; Kevin C. Cox/Getty Images Sport/Getty Images, 24; Richard Paul Kane/Shutterstock Images, 27; Melissa Tamez/Icon Sportswire/AP Images, 28; Jae C. Hong/AP Images, 29; Jeff Chiu/AP Images, 30, 117; Ellen Schmidt/AP Images, 31; Andrew Will/Shutterstock Images, 33; Elise Amendola/AP Images, 35, 72; Eric Gay/AP Images, 36; Jerry Holt/Star Tribune/AP Images, 37; Brandon Dill/AP Images, 38; Christian Peterson/Getty Images Sport/Getty Images, 39, 71, 86; Mark Fann/Shutterstock Images, 40; Bebeto Matthews/AP Images, 42; HUM Images/Universal Images Group/Getty Images, 43; Underwood Archives/Archive Photos/Getty Images, 44; NCAA Photos/Getty Images, 46; AP Images, 47; Bettmann/Getty Images, 48, 54, 98, 99, 114; Minnesota Historical Society/Corbis Historical/Getty Images, 50; Hector Mata/AFP/Getty Images, 52–53; Icon Sportswire/Getty Images, 55; Ray Stubblebine/AP Images, 56; Tim Clayton/Corbis Sport/Getty Images, 57; ABDO Publishing, 59, 63; Scott Strazzante/San Francisco Chronicle/AP Images, 60; Michael Conroy/AP Images, 64, 112; M. Anthony Nesmith/Icon Sportswire/Getty Images, 65; D. Myles Cullen/US Department of Defense, 66; Nell Redmond/AP Images, 67, 97; Tom Pennington/Getty Images Sport/Getty Images, 68; Michael Stravato/AP Images for Allstate/AP Images, 69; Jamie Squire/Getty Images Sport/Getty Images, 70–71; Focus on Sport/Getty Images Sport/Getty Images, 73; Focus on Sport/Getty Images, 74, 80, 90, 100, 102, 105, 115; Bob Riha Jr./Archive Photos/Getty Images, 75; Fred Jewell/AP Images, 77; David Zalubowski/AP Images, 78; Stan Honda/AFP/Getty Images, 79; Paul Sancya/AP Images, 81; David J. Phillip/AP Images, 82; Brett Coomer/AP Images, 83; Lorie Shaull/Flickr, 84, 85, 120, 122; Chris O'Meara/AP Images, 87; Associated Students of the University of California at Los Angeles, 88; Chris Graythen/Getty Images Sport/Getty Images, 89; Darron Cummings/AP Images, 91; Charlie Riedel/AP Images, 92; Matthew Holst/Getty Images Sport/Getty Images, 93; Damian Strohmeyer/Allsport/Hulton Archive/Getty Images, 94; Joe Robbins/Getty Images Sport/Getty Images, 95; Cody Glenn/Icon Sportswire/Getty Images, 96; Mike Powell/Getty Images Sport/Getty Images, 103; Pat Sullivan/AP Images, 107, 118; Mark J. Terrill/AP Images, 108, 109; Gregory Shamus/Getty Images Sport/Getty Images, 110; Ezra Shaw/Getty Images Sport/Getty Images, 111; Erik Drost/Wikimedia Commons, 113; Paul Buck/AFP/Getty Images, 116; Jeff Gross/Allsport/Getty Images Sport/Getty Images, 119; Tom Hood/AP Images, 121; Charles Krupa/AP Images, 123; Rob Carr/Getty Images Sport/Getty Images, 124; Chase Stevens/AP Images, 125